Hello English!

Contents

The rights of the language learner

Learning English is a really fun thing to do. You might know some of the words in this book already or you might never have seen them before.

Here are a few tips for you to remember as you practise the words you know and learn new ones.

1.
The right to have a go

2.
The right to make mistakes

3.

The right not to pronounce perfectly

4.

The right to make friends with someone who doesn't speak your language

5.

The right to ask someone to repeat

Can you think of any others?

This is me...

Start with the most important person: **you!** Learn how to tell other people your name and your age. Then ask them their name and how old they are. These are the first steps to making a new friend in English.

one	six	eleven	sixteen
two	seven	twelve	seventeen
three	eight	thirteen	eighteen
four	nine	fourteen	nineteen
five	ten	fifteen	twenty

I am eight years old.

How old are you?

I am six years old.

Hello!

These words and phrases will help you to greet people in English.
Practise saying hello and goodbye in English with your friends or family.
Ask them how they are, too!

me	him	her
you	us	them

My family

Read about the families on this page then describe your own family. Try telling someone else about your family or, for an extra challenge, write about your family in sentences. Use the words in the box opposite to help you.

This is my dad. His name is Ben.
He is wearing a T-shirt.

Use these words to talk about people

I			you	*(the same for a single person or more than one person)*
he	she	we	they	
brother/sister			grandfather/grandmother	

This is my mum.
Her name is Mary.
She is wearing a shirt.

At home

tree

nest

garage

hedge

ball

path

Garden

worm

flower

chimney

House

roof

window

fence

door

bin

ladder

hose pipe

grass

The kitchen and the living room

knife

fridge

cupboard

oven

Kitchen

spoon

sink

fork

stairs

telephone

sofa

cushion

television

cup of tea

coffee

armchair

Living room

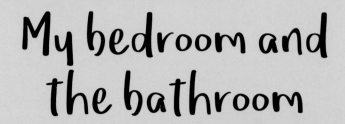

My bedroom and the bathroom

shower

mirror

toothbrush

toothpaste

sink

toilet

soap

bath

Bathroom

towel

curtains

wardrobe

poster

alarm clock

Bedroom

chest of drawers

colouring book

bed

doll

crafts

football boots

ballet shoes

The town

train

post office

fire engine

car

motorbike

taxi

Town

police car

aeroplane

train station

cinema

car park

hospital

town hall

ambulance

bus

Vehicles

At the supermarket

till

fishmonger

butcher

seafood

meat

shopping basket

vegetables

Supermarket

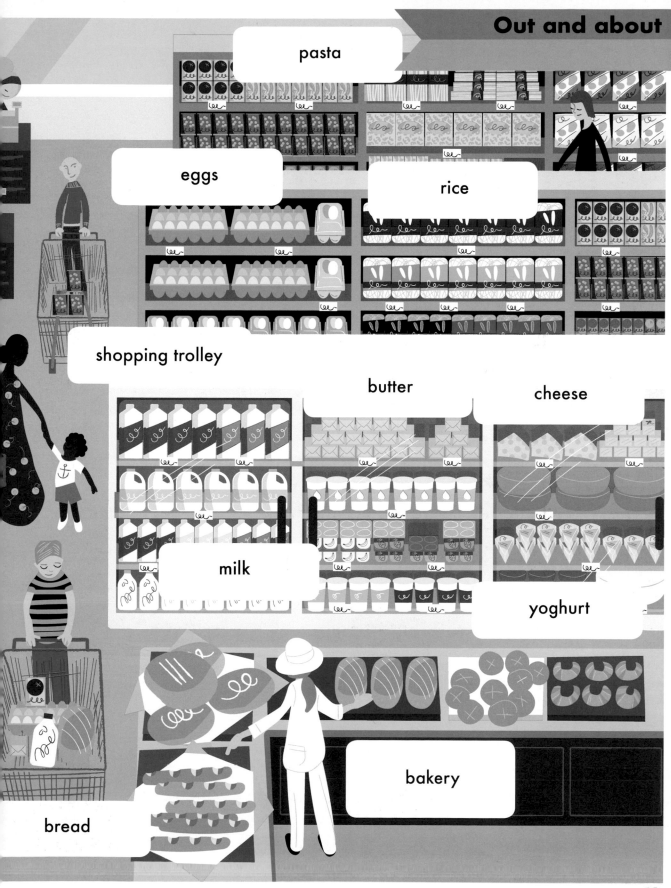

pasta

eggs

rice

shopping trolley

butter

cheese

milk

yoghurt

bakery

bread

My favourite foods

It's great to try new food but there are some foods we like more than others. Try these phrases out with your family at meal times to explain what tastes good and what you're not so keen on.

I like bananas!

I don't like grapes!

Do you like ice cream?

I love

I hate

favourite

apple

orange

Yes! I really like mint chocolate ice cream.

Do you like pizza?

No, I prefer pasta.

Use these words to talk about food

strawberry	broccoli	chips
raspberry	carrot	sausage
pear	green beans	cake
peach	fruit	chicken
tomato	sweetcorn	mashed potato

At the park

swan

skateboard

bridge

bench

baseball

football

kite

river

bird

duck

Park

tennis

basketball

gymnastics

bicycle

rugby

Sport

ice cream

dog

squirrel

Opposites

In this woodland, the animals are helping to show you some words and their opposites. Can you find the pairs of opposites that go together? You can use the opposites to help you compare things.

The deer is big.

The mouse is under the leaf.

The hedgehog is low down.

The ladybird is on top of the stone.

Use these handy phrases to compare things

The bird is inside but the squirrel is outside.

The caterpillar is smaller than the deer.

The owl is very high up.

The squirrel is outside.

The owl is high up.

The bird is inside.

The caterpillar is small.

Did you match the pairs correctly?

high up – low down   big – small   inside – outside   under – on top of

I would like...

Picnics are great fun! To make sure everyone gets what they want, you'll need to share. Practise these words and phrases so you can ask for what you want and offer food to your friends.

Use these handy phrases to share things

I have enough.	It's too much!	It's a lot.	Do you want some more bread?

Do you want a sandwich?

Yes, I'd like one.

Shall we share a cake?

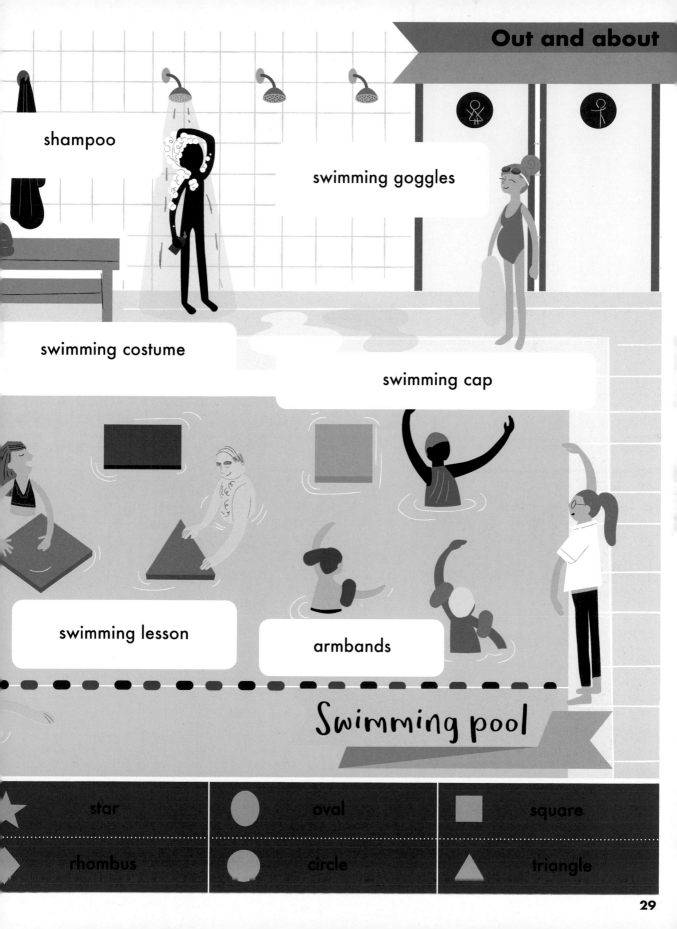

shampoo

swimming goggles

swimming costume

swimming cap

swimming lesson

armbands

Swimming pool

★	star		oval		square
	rhombus		circle		triangle

At the library

stories

shelf

comic

pirate

witch

fairy

unicorn

mermaid

knight

princess

once upon a time...

storytime

dragon

librarian

castle

computer

Library

Getting around

It's important to know how to ask for directions, especially when you're somewhere new. Learn these words and phrases to make sure you never get lost! You can use them to chat to people about how you get around, too.

Excuse me.

How do I get to the library?

Turn right. It's opposite.

Is the park far?

No, it's very near.

Which way?

on the left

on the right

straight on

next to

in front of

by train

by car

where is it?

over there

here

At school

whiteboard

calendar

alphabet

pen

teaching assistant

glue

scissors

chair

answer

repeat

look

listen

clock

teacher

book

desk

paper

paints

Classroom

colouring pencil

What time is it?

At what time do you get up? Have lunch? Go to bed? It's handy to know the right words to ask the time or explain when you do things. Try out some of these useful words and phrases to talk about your day.

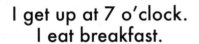

I get up at 7 o'clock.
I eat breakfast.

I eat lunch at school at midday.

Learn the days of the week

Monday	Wednesday
Tuesday	Thursday

I go home at quarter past three. I eat a snack.

I eat dinner with my family at half past six.

I go to bed at quarter to eight. Sleep well!

Friday	Sunday	yesterday
Saturday	today	tomorrow

Friends from around the world!

It's great to meet people from different parts of the world. You can learn about other countries and what life is like there, and you can tell your new friends what it's like where you live. These words and phrases will help you.

I come from England. It's in Europe.

She comes from Chile. It's in South America.

Where are you from?

He comes from Mali. It's in Africa.

Do you speak English?

No, I speak French.

Yes, I speak English and I speak Hindi as well.

The world

North America

Australia

South Africa

Asia

Antarctica

New Zealand

world

continent

language

country

The body

The words and phrases on these pages are all about our bodies. Use them to describe your appearance, say when you've hurt yourself or even play Simon Says!

Other parts of the body

mouth	arm	leg	shoulders
ears	elbow	foot	hair
lips	finger	toes	eyes

> Where does it hurt?

> I've hurt my knee.

> My tummy hurts.

> Simon says touch your nose.

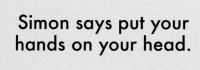

> Simon says put your hands on your head.

Playing

climbing

skipping

hiding

carrying

pushing

running

hugging

Playground

sitting

shouting

singing

reading

standing

dancing

jumping

throwing

walking

pulling

What is he doing?

What is she doing?

Happy birthday!

excited

angry

hungry

thirsty

cake

sweets

milkshake

chocolate

biscuit

Emotions

happy

surprised

sad

shy

tired

pizza

Party

When is your birthday?

My birthday is on...

Come to my party!

I feel...

birthday card

birthday present

Weather

Do you like sunny days, splashing in puddles or throwing snowballs? Learn these words and phrases to describe what it's like outside, whatever the weather, and say what you do in each season of the year.

In the spring...

It's raining and it's cloudy.

I'm wearing my wellingtons and my raincoat.

In the summer...

It's a sunny day. It's hot!

Let's go on a bug hunt!

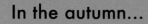

In the autumn...

Let's fly a kite!

It's windy. I'm wearing my coat and he's wearing his scarf.

It's snowing and it's cold.

I'm wearing my hat and my gloves.

In the winter...

Months

January

February

March

April

May

June

July

August

September

October

November

December

At the zoo

bear

tiger

lion

gazelle

kangaroo

zookeeper

tortoise

hippopotamus

elephant

rhinoceros

crocodile

giraffe

cheetah

How many trees can you see?

parrot

snake

visitor

At the beach

sky

Beach

sand

beach umbrella

surfboard

sun cream

shell

spade

bucket

lighthouse

seagull

wave

boat

Sea

seaweed

rock

sand castle

Under the sea

What colour is it?

Colours

⬤	red
⬤	black
⬤	yellow
⬤	orange
⬤	brown
⬤	green
⬤	purple
⬤	white
⬤	blue

coral

shipwreck

crab

dolphin

diver

octopus

fish

whale

shark

Ocean

lobster

At the farm

field

donkey

calf

sheep

hay

lamb

hen

rooster

Farm

chick

barn

horse

foal

cow

pig

farmer

rabbit

piglet

cat

goat

mouse

Word List

A
aeroplane
Africa
alarm clock
alphabet
ambulance
angry
Antarctica
apple
April
answer
arm
armbands
armchair
Asia
August
Australia
autumn

B
bakery
ball
ballet shoes
banana
barn
baseball
basketball
bath
bathroom
beach
beach umbrella
bear
bed
bedroom
bench
bicycle
big
bike
bin
bird
birthday
birthday cake
birthday card
birthday present

biscuit
black
blonde
blue
boat
body
book
bread
breakfast
bridge
broccoli
brother
brown
bucket
bug hunt
bus
but
butcher
butter

C
cake
calendar
calf
car
car park
carrot
carry
castle
cat
caterpillar
chair
cheese
cheetah
chest of drawers
chick
Chile
chimney
chips
chocolate
cinema
circle
classroom

climb
clock
clothes
cloudy
coat
coffee
cold
colouring book
colouring pencil
colours
comic
computer
continent
coral
country
cow
crab
crafts
crisps
crocodile
cup of tea
cupboard
curly
curtains
cushion

D
dad
dance
day
December
deer
desk
dinner
directions
diver
diving board
dog
doll
dolphin
donkey
door
dragon

duck
ears
Earth
eggs
eight
eighteen
elbow
elephant
eleven
emotions
England
English
enough
Europe
evening
excited
eyes
fairy
family
far
farm
farmer
favourite
February
fence
field
fifteen
finger
fire engine
fish
fishmonger
five
flower
foal
food
foot
football
football boots
fork
four
fourteen

French
Friday
fridge
fruit
G garage
garden
gazelle
giraffe
gloves
glue
goat
goodbye
goodnight
grandfather
grandmother
grapes
grass
green
green beans
gymnastics
H hair
hand
happy
hat
hay
he
head
hedge
hedgehog
hello
hen
her
here
hexagon
hi
hide
high
him
Hindi
hippopotamus
horse

hose pipe
hospital
hot
house
hug
hungry
I I
ice cream
inside
J January
July
jump
June
K kangaroo
kitchen
kite
knee
knife
knight
L ladder
ladybird
lamb
language
leaf
left
leg
librarian
library
lifeguard
lighthouse
lion
lips
listen
living room
lobster
long
look
low
lunch
M Mali
March

Word List

mashed potato
May
me
meat
mermaid
midday
milk
milkshake
mirror
Monday
more
morning
motorbike
mouse
mouth
mum

N near
nest
New Zealand
next to
nine
nineteen
no
North America
nose
November

O ocean
October
octopus
on top
once upon a time
one
opposite
opposites
orange (colour)
orange (fruit)
outside
oval
oven
over there
owl

P paints
paper
park
parallelogram
parrot
party
pasta
path
peach
pear
pen
pentagon
pig
piglet
pirate
pizza
playground
police car
post office
poster
princess
pulling
purple
push

R rabbit
raincoat
rain
raspberry
read
rectangle
red
repeat
rhinoceros
rhombus
rice
right
river
rock
roof
rooster
rugby

ruler
run

S sad
sand
sand castle
sandwich
Saturday
sausage
scarf
school
scissors
sea
seafood
seagull
seaweed
September
seven
seventeen
shampoo
share
shapes
shark
she
sheep
shelf
shell
shipwreck
shirt
shopping basket
shopping trolley
shoulders
shouting
South America
shower
shy
sing
sink
sister
sit
six
sixteen

skateboard
skip
sky
small
snack
snake
snow
soap
sofa
South Africa
spade
spoon
sport
spring
square
squirrel
stairs
stand
straight on
stone
star
stories
storytime
strawberry
summer
sun cream
Sunday
sunny
supermarket
surfboard
surprised
swan
sweetcorn
sweets
swimming
swimming cap
swimming costume
swimming goggles
swimming lesson
swimming pool
taxi

teacher
telephone
television
ten
tennis
them
they
thirsty
thirteen
three
throw
Thursday
tiger
till
time
tired
today
toes
toilet
tomato
tomorrow
too much
toothbrush
toothpaste
tortoise
towel
town
town hall
train
train station
tree
triangle
Tuesday
tummy
turn
twelve
twenty
two
U under
underwater
unicorn

us
V vegetables
vehicles
visitor
W walk
wardrobe
wave
we
weather
Wednesday
well (feeling)
wellingtons
whale
where
white
whiteboard
windy
window
winter
witch
world
worm
y yellow
yes
yesterday
yoghurt
you
Z zoo
zookeeper

Phrase List

Greetings & conversation

excuse me

good evening

good morning

happy birthday

here is

here you go!

I'm well

please

thank you

Giving information

a lot

brown/blue/green eyes

come to my party

he comes from

he is wearing

her name is

he's called

his name is

I am

I come from

I don't like

I get up

I go

I go to bed

I hate

I have

I have enough

I like

I love

I prefer

I speak

I wear

I would like

in front of

it is

it's a lot

it's too much

I've hurt myself

my birthday is on

my name is

red/blonde/black/brown hair

she comes from

she is wearing

she's called

Simon says

the most

this is

_____ years old

Asking questions

do you like?

do you speak?

do you want?

how are you?

how do I get to?

how many?

how old are you?

shall we?

what colour is it?

what is he doing?

what is she doing?

what is your name?

what's the weather like?

when is your birthday?

Telling the time

half past

one/two/three/four o'clock

quarter past

quarter to

Describing the weather

it's cold

it's hot

it's snowing/raining

it's sunny

Notes for parents

We hope you and your children or pupils enjoy exploring the English words and phrases in this book together. We have included vocabulary from everyday situations, and places that will be familiar to younger children, to support them as they take their first steps in English language learning.

On some pages, you will find vocabulary to learn with your child. This is accompanied by illustrations to help your child understand the meaning of new words. On other pages, you'll find complete sentences so that you and your child can practise asking and answering questions, and having conversations, as their confidence grows.

At the back of the book is a list of key words from the different pages of the book. These are arranged alphabetically to help you find what you are looking for. There is also a list of useful phrases, which is organised into sections.

Here are a few suggestions for using the book:

- Start with a page that only includes vocabulary. Ask your child in their native language to find something in the illustration so that they become familiar with the content of the page. If you are reading the book with more than one child, turn this into a game by seeing who can be the first to spot the different things. Or play a game of 'I spy'!

- Go back to the same page the next time you read the book. This time, tell the child the word in English when they find what you've asked them to hunt for. Don't worry if your pronunciation isn't quite correct. Just have fun trying out the words. It is important that the child can see you having a go even if you are unsure. This will reassure them that imperfection is OK when you start to learn a new language. Let your child concentrate on listening to the words at this stage instead of trying to read them or even speak them themselves.

- The next time you play this game, see if the child can repeat the English words back to you. They'll still need lots of opportunities to listen to the new English words, so try to say each word at least twice before the child has a go. Resist the temptation to correct their pronunciation – instead, praise them for having a go and repeat the word back to them before you move on to a new piece of vocabulary. They will soon pick up how to say the English words.

- Eventually, you'll be able to ask the child in English to find things in the illustration or to point to something and ask them to tell you the English word.

- When you think you and the child are ready, move on to the pages with conversations on them. The ones at the start of the book are easier than the ones further on. Start by seeing if you can work out together what the characters on the pages might be saying to one another. Then read the conversations in English to the child. Once they have heard the

conversations a few times, they might be keen to join in with you. If not, don't worry. Just keep reading the conversations to them and they will join in when they're ready.

- Above all, encourage the child to have a go and give lots of praise. Younger children are usually quite unselfconscious and this is excellent for building up confidence in a foreign language.

written by Sam Hutchinson & Emilie Martin

illustrated by Kim Hankinson

Published by b small publishing ltd.

www.bsmall.co.uk

Text & Illustrations copyright © b small publishing ltd. 2018

1 2 3 4 5

ISBN 978-1-911509-73-8

Design: Kim Hankinson   Editorial: Emilie Martin & Rachel Thorpe   Production: Madeleine Ehm

Publisher: Sam Hutchinson

Printed in China by WKT Co. Ltd.